E. N. Wood

Guide to Santa Barbara Town and County

Containing information on matters of interest to tourists, new settlers,

invalids, etc.

E. N. Wood

Guide to Santa Barbara Town and County
Containing information on matters of interest to tourists, new settlers, invalids, etc.

ISBN/EAN: 9783337381974

Printed in Europe, USA, Canada, Australia, Japan

Cover: Foto ©Lupo / pixelio.de

More available books at **www.hansebooks.com**

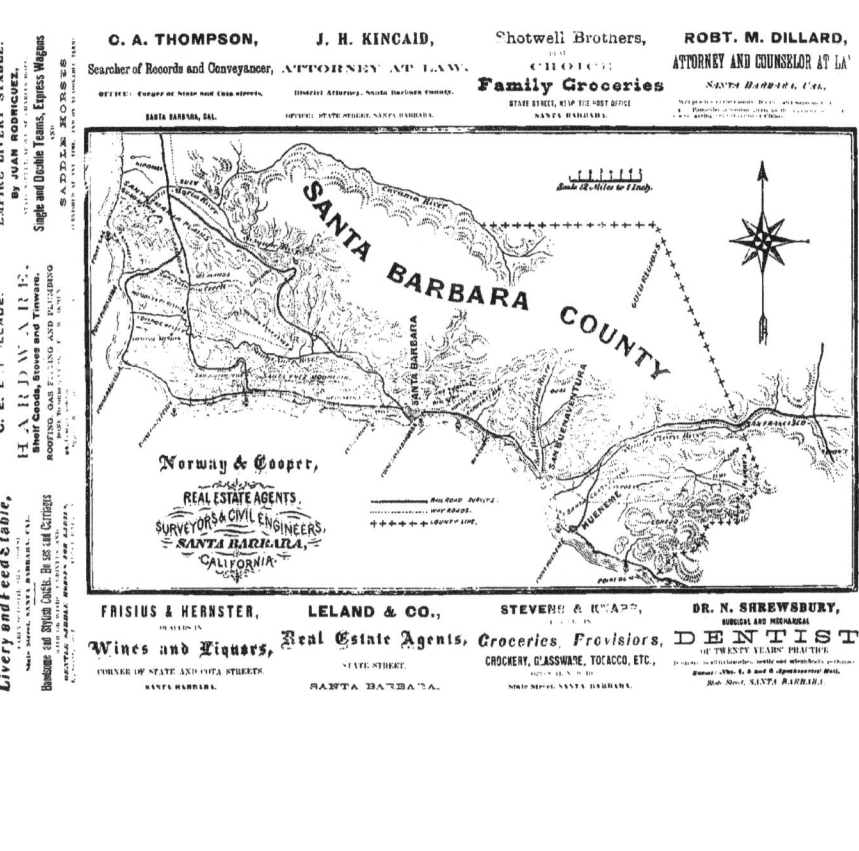

GUIDE

TO

SANTA BARBARA

TOWN AND COUNTY,

CONTAINING INFORMATION ON MATTERS OF INTEREST
TO TOURISTS, NEW SETTLERS, INVALIDS, ETC.

With an Accurate Map of the County,
Engraved Expressly for this Work.

By E. N. WOOD.

SANTA BARBARA, CAL.:
WOOD & SEFTON, BOOK AND JOB PRINTERS.
1872.

TABLE OF CONTENTS.

	PAGE.
1. Early History,	7
2. The Mission System,	8
3. Recent History,	9
4. Means of Access,	10
5. The Town,	12
6. Hotels,	13
7. Hacks, Carriages and Livery.	14
8. Gas and Water Companies.	15
9. Town Library,	15
10. Secret Societies,	16
11. Churches,	16
12. School Facilities,	17
13. Population,	19
14. Local Government,	20
15. Financial Condition,	20
16. Newspapers,	21
17. Other Towns,	21
18. Places of Interest to Visitors,	22

TABLE OF CONTENTS.

19. The Hot Springs,	24
20. The Mission,	24
21. The Mammoth Grapevine,	26
22. Colonel Hollister's,	28
23. Climate,	31
24. Climate for Invalids,	34
25. Temperature,	49
26. Scenery,	51
27. Fishing and Hunting,	53
28. Irrigation,	54
29. Agriculture,	55
30. Cheap House Building,	61
31. Fruit Culture,	62
32. Wool Growing,	68
33. Cost of Living,	69
34. Mineralogy,	71
35. Earthquakes,	72
36. California and Palestine,	74
37. The Valley of Santa Barbara,	75

TO THE READER.

This little work does not pretend to be largely original. The class of people whom it is intended more especially to interest, are more concerned to find it trustworthy than original, and we have endeavored to meet their wishes. It is mainly a compilation of facts and reports of disinterested persons with regard to this portion of California, most of which are things familiar to our home readers, but no less new and interesting to visitors and those who think of settling here. The materials have been carefully and conscientiously selected, and we believe every important statement we have made has been pronounced within bounds by competent judges in each specialty. We have given copious extracts from letters of intelligent visitors, not from want of other material, but on account of the added authority furnished in most instances by the names of the writers.

Let us go to Santa Barbara !—The descriptions that come from there are enchanting as well as appetizing. Olive and orange groves; stately walnut trees: vines clustering on the hill-side; fruits of every variety—tropical, semi-tropical, and temperate; orchards equaling those of Sorrento, and an air from the ocean as soft and refreshing as from the Mediterranean. Beach drives unequaled; mountain views unrivaled; romantic glens and groves.—*Harper's Bazar*.

SANTA BARBARA.

EARLY HISTORY.

THE earliest authentic record states that California was discovered in 1542, fifty years after Columbus landed upon San Salvador, by Cabrillo, a navigator in the Spanish service. He spent six months among the natives in what is now Santa Barbara county, and has left on record the names of forty towns or villages which then existed in this section of the state. Our county has an antiquity of its own. Three hundred years ago it was a densely populated region; its fertile soil freely supplied nuts and wild fruits; native horses roamed over its hills, and abundant game of many kinds since exterminated; the bay swarmed with fish. The simple and indolent aborigines wore no clothing to speak of, all their needs were supplied by nature and the delicious climate, they lived out their days in security and unconcern, and handed down through the years their traditions and tropical mythology. On Catalina Island was a temple containing an idol which was worshiped with sacrifices.

The whole country swarmed with a population vastly greater than has since occupied it. At long intervals huge ships appeared upon the quiet bay and strange-tongued men came ashore, procured supplies and sailed away. And as the years passed on, the coming of the strange ships grew more frequent, till it gradually became known to the explorers that California was not an island, and was not a peninsula, and the great river to the north did not connect with the Atlantic ocean.

But alas! as the knowledge of the stranger grew, and his footsteps encroached upon their territory, the primitive race slowly faded before him. Their day had passed into the twilight when, a hundred years ago, the Catholic religion and the Spanish arms gained a foothold among them.

THE MISSION SYSTEM.

The first efforts toward civilization were made by the Franciscan friars. They founded the first Mission in California at San Diego in 1769. That of Santa Barbara was established in 1786, being the tenth in point of time. Here they gathered the natives, taught them the mysteries of religion and labor, and fed them on rice and moral precepts. After a few years of toil and privation the Holy Fathers began to grow into power and opulence. They were the temporal as well as spiritual lords of the land; they cultivated the vine, the olive and the fig, and enjoyed all the comforts and luxuries a genial climate, a generous soil and abundance of costless labor could produce; for the whole race of natives were their servants, working for food and raiment of their own production. For sixty years, or until 1830, the missionaries had an almost undisturbed field in which to test their schemes for civilizing the natives. They extended their dominion from San Diego to San Francisco, establishing Missions at intervals of twenty or thirty miles, and appropriating the lands between, so that the coast was lined with a cordon of their contiguous possessions. They founded in all twenty Missions, the last in 1820. From 1800 to 1822 (when the Spanish dominion in Mexico was overthrown), the Fathers appear to have experienced the halcyon days of their system, living in patriarchal state with almost regal revenues and powers. In 1825 the Mission of Santa Barbara had 75,000 cattle, 5,000 tame horses and mules and 40,000 sheep. The immense wealth of the Missions proved their ruin. It became known in Mexico, and through the numerous revolutions occurring there, the Missions were regarded as lawful prey and every change of government brought them new despoilers. In 1840 the Mexican government took charge of them and most of them were allowed to go to decay. Thus ended the Mission system.

Its Recent History.

After the palmy days of the priestly rule had yielded to military and civil dominion, and allegiance had been transferred from Spain to Mexico, Santa Barbara was a place of importance in the territory. Here certain of the Governors resided, and here were held "Departmental Assemblies," till they went out in 1846 with Pio Pico, the last of the old-time Governors. So late as 1841 Los Angeles was the largest town in California, and Santa Barbara and San Francisco were of equal size. In 1846 the question of annexing California to England was discussed and decided in the negative at an "Assembly" convened in this town. Soon after this event the discovery of gold created new centres of wealth and population nearer the mining regions, and the southern portion of the state was left in quiet in the mad rush for speedier gains. Of late statistics show that only 16 per cent. of the gross products of the state arise from gold and other metals, and 45 per cent. from agricultural sources, and this section increases in importance more than correspondingly; for its soil is by no means the only ground on which it now receives such ready and wide spread notice.

Means of Access.

It is reached from San Francisco by the steamers of the Pacific Mail Steamship Company, the "Kalorama." of another line, or overland by railroad and stage. As one comes down the coast the change in atmosphere and climate is as marked when he has passed Point Concepcion as when he has passed Cape Hatteras on the Atlantic coast. The weather becomes warm and bright; those who were seasick come on deck and all find constant pleasure in admiring the wild and picturesque scenery of the Coast Range of mountains which closely follows the trend of the shore for most of the way. Through nearly the whole trip the vessel sails within sight of the land,—so near indeed as often to render easily discernible houses and fences and grazing cattle, where the mountains recede a little, leaving fertile and beautiful valleys bordering on the water.

During the rains and the earlier months of summer these seaside valleys form most beautiful pictures, their bright shades of green contrasting so vividly with the black mountain sides and the level waste of waters on the other side of the ship. Thirty hours out from the Golden Gate, the steamer, turning a sudden point, faces directly north and comes up the bay to the anchorage. Before it spreads the town of Santa Barbara, half hidden among its trees, low and cool and beautiful in the peculiar film of the sunset that seems to fill all the air with floating gold. The waters of the bay are still and level as a floor, and few scenes are fairer than this which spreads itself out to the traveler standing on the deck.

Those who prefer travaling on *terra firma* can take the cars of the San Jose railroad from San Francisco to Gilroy, whence the journey is finished by daily stages. It is now almost positive that the Atlantic and Pacific railroad will pass through Santa Barbara, when it will become an important point on a great continental route, easily reached from any quarter.

THE TOWN.

It is situated on the sea, nearly in the centre of the county, on the southern coast line. It extends for a mile and a half back from the beach. Many houses of the Spanish population are of adobe, roofed with red semi-cylindrical tiles in the old style of southern Spain.

" Santa Barbara has one of the most beautiful situations in California, placed in a green valley opening out to the sea, between picturesque hills on either side, and with a fine chain of mountains in the back ground. The grand old Spanish Mission seems to stand guard over it, upon the hills behind."—[The New West, by C. L. Brace.

" Impartially viewed in its surroundings, and for natural advantages, Santa Barbara is the most delightful place in California. The town stands on gently rising ground, and is well laid out with broad avenues. Skirting the beach, its plateau extends back about three miles, and possesses many beautiful sites for residences. Its gradual slope is also ample for drainage. Viewed from the sea its panorama is one of great beauty. Prosperity and good taste are exhibited in the style of its new buildings."—[Correspondence San Francisco Examiner.

The environs of the town are being rapidly built up with tasteful and pleasant houses, and the buildings indicate that the attainment of solid comfort has been the object of their owners. Each year gives us more

and better new buildings than any previous one. Durthe year ending October, buildings have been finished
or begun in the town, the aggregate cost of which will
amount to $200,000. A good deal of real estate is
changing hands, not only in town but through the
county. The value of all property is increasing steadily and normally. It is no mushroom growth. New
comers are buying lots and erecting houses for homes,
not for speculation.

HOTELS.

The leading hotel is the Shaw House. It is a large
three story brick building, on the corner of State and
Haley streets. Incorporated in the brick work is a
solid frame work of timber which was first put up,
braced and anchored in the strongest manner, to give
firmness to the structure. Broad verandas front on the
two streets, and the rooms are handsomely furnished,
pleasant and sunny. Mr. Shaw is an accommodating
landlord, and the house is well kept and generally full
of guests. It was completed in the autumn of 1871.
The transient charge is $2 00 per day.

The St. Charles is a two-story adobe building, surrounded by verandas above and below, in appropriate
style for this climate. Its table is good and charges
are $1 50 to $2 00 per day. It is reported that this
house is soon to be very greatly enlarged and improved.

A new hotel, the largest in town, is nearly completed

and will be opened in November. It is on the corner of State and Cota streets, and presents an imposing appearance, being three stories high, with Mansard roof, observatory and verandas. It is of brick, the principal material now used in the construction of stores and public buildings. It is supplied with all the modern improvements and Mr. Raffour promises to make it a' strictly first-class house, as he is capable of doing. It will contain billiard rooms, telegraph office, barber's saloon, &c. Charges are not yet fixed but will be moderate.

For such as wish to live more quietly there are several excellent boarding houses. Among them we may mention those of E. J. Knapp and D. E. Ver Planck, which are convenient to the beach, and A. L. Lincoln's up town and in dryer air.

HACKS, CARRIAGES AND LIVERY.

The facilities for conveyance about the town and to the various places of interest in the vicinity are most ample. Carriages, open and close, are always in front of the hotels, and as good as can be found anywhere. Their owners usually drive them, and are interested in giving satisfaction to customers. The charges to or from the steamers is 50 cents. For driving about the town $2 an hour.

The livery stables furnish excellent turnouts, and drivers if desired. Their rates are:

Saddle horse per day..$2 00

Single carriage per day..$5 00
" " half day or less.. 2 50
Two horse carriage per day...................................... 7 00
" " half day.. 4 00

No visitor who does not take several drives in different directions from the town, can have an adequate idea of the natural beauty of this vicinity.

We have no street railroad as yet, but a passenger-express wagon runs up and down State street during the day, in which one may ride the length of the town for an eight cent ticket.

GAS AND WATER COMPANIES.

The Maxim Gas Company put up works in town a few months since, and their pipes have been introduced into a number of public and private houses, besides lighting State street.

Within a few months the town will be supplied with water in pipes. Portions of the necessary works were constructed long ago by the Indians attached to the Mission, and consist of reservoirs and aqueducts running over with pure spring water from the neighboring hills. The lower reservoir has a capacity of 1,500,000 gallons.

THE LIBRARY.

This is one of the features of the place. Several hundred carefully selected books are collected and new publications are constantly added. It is a pleasant and popular resort among reading people, and is something rarely found in Western towns of this size. Its origin and continuance are due to the energetic efforts of a young lady who came here for her health two years since.

SOCIETIES.

The Masons and Odd Fellows have flourishing chapters here, which meet in rooms over the store of F. W. Frost & Co. The Santa Barbara Lodge, No. 192, F. and A. M. meets every fourth Saturday evening.

Santa Barbara Lodge No. 156, I. O. O. F. meets on Tuesday evenings at 8 o'clock.

CHURCHES.

The town is well supplied with churches, all of which have settled preachers and are in a prosperous condition. Besides the Mission, which is still opened for services, there are five others. The Catholic is the largest, of which most of the Mexican and some of the older American settlers are members. It is centrally located on State street and has a chime of bells swung in the yard which were cast in Spain. The building is 100 feet long with an addition of forty feet for the altar. Its pastor is a native of Spain, a man of great zeal and energy and of courtly manners. The congregation is large and the music fine. Services are conducted in English and Spanish.

The Episcopal church is near the hotels and the beach. It is a brick building, plainly fitted up. The congregation is not large but steadily increasing. The ladies of the church have just built and furnished a parsonage.

The Methodist church, corner Vine and De la Guerra streets, is of brick, neat and of good size. The parsonage stands next the church. Pastor, Rev. Robert Bentley.

The Presbyterians occupy a very neat frame chapel, one block from the Methodist, preparatory to erecting a handsome church. It is generally quite filled on Sunday mornings, and is under the pastoral care of Rev. J. Phelps, D.D.

The Congregational church is the most pretentious of these structures. It is of brick, in the Gothic style, with a handsome tower on one corner, and an attractive interior.

School Facilities.

There are some twenty school districts in the county; female teachers are in demand and earn from $50 to $100 a month, but they need to be well qualified in order to pass the preliminary examination, which is stricter than at the East. The school houses are better built and furnished than they will average in New England, in counties of equal population.

The Public School house in Santa Barbara is a

handsome two-story brick building with high basement, recently finished at a cost of $12,500 and surrounded with ample grounds. The rooms are spacious and well ventilated. Those on each floor are connected by huge sliding doors to allow of their being thrown into one room when desired. This structure is occupied by the higher departments of the Public Schools, and is so planned that its capacity can be doubled, as will soon become necessary, by joining to it a duplicate structure. It is liberally supplied with maps and the usual accessories now common, and is fitted up with the latest styles of furniture. It also has a well selected though not yet large library.

The Santa Barbara College was established in 1869 as a high school with a regular course of study. It has prospered so beyond expectation that already the large building is found insufficient for its needs, and the Board of Trustees are now adding large extensions to the edifice, and at the same time greatly enlarging the scope of the course of study. Among the improvements is a fine and complete Gymnasium. They have an accomplished corps of teachers headed by a graduate of a celebrated German University. This school bids fair to become one of the most popular and thorough in California.

The Franciscan College (Catholic) was founded in 1868. It occupies the wing of the Mission building. From 80 to 100 boys are educated here every year at little more than half the expense in most schools of the state. This institution is very popular and it will soon become necessary to enlarge its accommodations.

The St. Vincent's School was established here by the Sisters of Charity, in 1858. Their present large building was completed in 1869. The increasing population of the town for the past three years having considerably augmented the number of pupils, it was deemed advisable to complete and improve the original plan of the building. This work is now progressing and when finished will add greatly to the comfort of the inmates. The grounds are spacious, and (except the recreation yard) under cultivation. Every branch of a thorough English, Spanish, French and musical education is taught by the Sisters.

Population.

The population of the town is about 3,500; of the county about 10,000. It is mainly composed of Americans; there is a large Spanish element, but it is gradually decreasing. The immigration is mostly from the North Atlantic and Western states, consisting of intelligent and educated people. Every year marks a steady and rapid increase of population, many of the new comers having acquired property elsewhere, being attracted here by the climate, from places where failing health of some member of the family, or the severity of the winters rendered their further residence undesirable.

LOCAL GOVERNMENT.

The machinery of our local government is very simple and inexpensive. County affairs are managed by a Board of Supervisors consisting of three members, and those of the city by a Common Council consisting of five members.

FINANCIAL CONDITION.

The indebtedness of the county is now $19,000, having been reduced one half since 1867, and is funded at the low rate of seven per cent. interest. On the other hand during the last five years the population of the county has *doubled*, and the assessed value of its real estate and personal property has increased *nearly tenfold*. During the same period the rate of taxation for county purposes has been reduced from two per cent. to six-tenths of one per cent. The value of real estate and personal property in 1870, according to the Census, was over $10,000,000. Only four other counties in the state have an equally small rate of taxation, and in those four the climate is worse, if possible, than taxes. Only two other counties have a climate similar to ours—Los Angeles and San Diego,—and both are saddled with an enormous county debt. This exhibit is by no means the least among the advantages offered by this county to settlers, and shows that its financial affairs have been carefully and faithfully administered.

NEWSPAPERS.

There are four newspaper offices in the county. The INDEX, *Press* and *Times* are published at Santa Barbara, and the *Signal* at San Buenaventura.

OTHER TOWNS.

San Buenaventura, thirty miles east of Santa Barbara, on the sea shore, is the next largest town in the county. The road between the two places is very romantic, running for half the distance along the narrow beach, between the ocean and almost perpendicular mountains. Ventura, as it is generally called, is also the site of one of the ancient Missions. It is a prosperous town and is steadily growing. A long wharf has recently been completed, and a large shipping business is done here, as it is the outlet for the products of hundreds of square miles of fertile agricultural country. The town is abundantly supplied with excellent water by a canal seven miles in length.

From Ventura eastward the mountains and coast line diverge nearly at right angles, and the country opens out into the broad rolling valleys containing some of the finest land in the state. In these valleys irrigation is practiced to quite an extent.

Hueneme (pronounced and sometimes spelled Wynema) is a sea-port town recently founded, fifteen miles below Ventura. It is accessible to sailing vessels and steamers, and the conformation of the shore is such that an ample and safe harbor can be constructed without an extravagant outlay. As Thos. A. Scott, the railroad king, owns an immense amount of land in this part of the county, including the town site, those who choose to settle here can be assured that intelligent management and immense resources will be employed in developing the country and building up an important town. A railroad from Hueneme through the valley of the Santa Clara river to Los Angeles is not an improbable thing in the near future.

There are several small villages or settlements in different parts of the county, of which we cannot give an extended notice for want of space.

Places of Interest to Visitors.

There are several places in town, or within easy distance of it, which those who travel for pleasure or instruction will find quite worthy of a visit for one reason or another. To one who thoughtfully studies what is here presented to his attention, the traditions and mythology of the past form a curious intermingling with the matter-of-fact existence of to-day.

At the orchards and vineyards of Mr. Goux and Mr. Packard, just west of town, may be seen a fair specimen of what our soil and climate will accomplish in the rapid maturity and prolific bearing of various fruits. Here also the silk-worm business and the processes of wine-making are open to the inspection of the stranger.

The grounds of Dr. Shaw and Judge Fernald are delightful places for one to study who doubts the wonderful capacities of this almost fairy land. In these grounds are fruit trees as follows: Apple, pear, peach, nectarine, apricot, fig (several varieties), Japan loquat, guava, lemon, orange, pomegranate, olive, English walnut, black walnut, Italian chestnut, almond. Among the shrubs and ornamental trees are the elm, locust, pepper, eucalyptus of many varieties, auricaria, fir, Monterey, Haytian and Italian cypress, Australian palm, laurustine, pongia and others. In addition these places, like many others, are bursting with beautiful and fragrant flowers such as a breath of frost would wither, but which here grow to mammoth size, and are perennial.

The beach is hard and smooth as a floor and affords a charming drive for many miles; and the views are successively lovely as we round each curve and point. Returning at sunset the scene is magnificent, the vessels rolling lazily on the water, the town spreading away under branching trees, the brilliant colors of the evening sky, and the warm, fresh, beautiful air that never chills and never enervates, while the huge billows break at our feet, and we seem floating rather than driving in the white borders of the sea.

One of the finest places in the vicinity of the town is that of Mr. Bond, in Montecito, which three years ago was covered with rocks and oak trees. It is now a smooth and well-kept almond orchard containing several hundred trees, besides fruit trees of various kinds.

The flower garden is filled with flowers and shrubs of rare varieties and from almost every latitude and country. The object of the owner is to ascertain what limits are imposed upon frigid or tropical vegetable growth by this climate. Several species of palm and the banana flourish beside firs and spruce trees. The alder, which is a shrub in New England, is here a tree thirty feet high. Geraniums and verbenas, which there grow in pots, here clamber over piazzas and cottage roofs.

The Hot Springs.

Up a steep winding road that bores like a corkscrew into the heart of the mountain, lie hidden away mineral springs of rare remedial power. The sick drink of the waters and bathe in them, and are healed. The well drive up of a morning, and go into the steaming pool of Siloam for pleasure. The scenery is rough and craggy and uncanny as the witches' cavern, but go out on one of those jutting rocks and you will look down upon a view that amply repays the exertion. The limited accommodations for invalid visitors at the springs are generally tasked to the utmost. A large hotel within a mile would never lack for patronage. The medicinal qualities of these waters will be referred to again.

The Mission.

The historical feature and nucleus of this old Mexican town, now in an active transition stage, is the old Mission Cathedral, about two miles from the wharves, and at about three hundred feet elevation above the sea level. It is usually the first object of interest to be visited by Eastern travelers. It is built of sandstone from the neighboring hills, and one is struck with the ancient grandeur of its imposing Moorish style of architecture. Its walls are over five feet in thickness, and the cement uniting them cannot be broken even with a heavy pick. They are further supported by heavy buttresses. It was built somewhat after the general plan of the other twenty on the coast. The church was the central object, and it was made as large and handsome as possible. Its interior was as highly decorated as the means of the Fathers would allow. The walls were covered with gorgeously colored paintings of objects calculated to attract the attention of the simple-minded natives, while about the altar were placed massive gilded candlesticks, images, gold and silver vessels, etc. Near the high altar are deposited the remains of the first bishop of Upper and Lower California, who died here. The *sombrero* of the prelate hangs above his tomb.

The Mission continues in good repair and is the most pretentious of these ancient structures. The main nave of the building is two hundred feet long and forty feet wide, having two high towers in front, with belfries of solid masonry, above each of which is the symbolical cross. To the left is a wing one hundred and thirty feet long, with porches supported by pillars and arches, all in a good state of preservation. This wing is now used for educational purposes. In front of this massive edifice there remain the ruins of a large fountain of ornate workmanship, and signs of the walks and *parterres* the worthy Padres delighted to cultivate. To one side is a large old olive orchard.

It is well known that the Fathers selected the choicest sites along the coast for their own use; it is evident they were men of sound judgment and clear sighted prophecy in many respects, and cultivated tastes. In the location of this Mission they were particularly happy; building stone, fuel and timber were abundant, and an inexhaustible supply of mountain water was close at hand; they were sufficiently removed from the sea to be secure from hostile attacks from that quarter, with such naval ordnance as was then in vogue, and on an eminence which swept the valley east and west for many miles; its white domes being the first object to meet the eye of the traveler, from whatever direction he might approach; the position was commanding, the soil rich and kindly, the scenery unsurpassed. The keen eyed Padres had marked the place on their frequent trips along the coast, both by land and sea, during the seventeen years they had been in the country. It is just beyond the town limits and is still opened for services performed by the Spanish pastor.

THE MAMMOTH GRAPEVINE.

Three miles east of the town, in Montecito, may be

seen the most gigantic grapevine in all the world. It is between fifty and seventy years old, as nearly as can be computed from the accounts given by the native people living about, and has grown from a slip stuck in the ground by a young Spanish woman who had cut it to use as a riding whip. The temptation is strong not to pass by this opportunity without weaving into the tradition some little romantic sketch, but want of space and romance compels us to resist it. The vine stands erect like the trunk of a large tree till it reaches the hight of eight feet, where it measures four feet and eight inches in circumference. Here it divides into several horizontal branches, each as large as a man's leg, which sub-divide and wind away and run riot over an immense trellis, covering an area of 4,000 square feet with a tangled thicket of green leaves and purple grapes, through which the fervid rays of a September sun never find their way.

Under this tropical trellis, on the hard beaten earth, many a rising moon has thrown its level beams upon señor and señorita dancing to the sad guitar, or upon the easy swing and wild abandon of the Spanish fandango. Here is the romance of the south. Here should the poet lounge and smoke in the starlight without, watching the dreamy convolutions of the waltz, listening to the soft rhythm of the Spanish tongue as voices float above the sighing of the music. Here too have come the murderer and the outlaw, stopping for pleasure in their flight from death. And here the officers of justice overtaking the fugitive, a desperate shot and its answer have interrupted the dance for a moment and put the desperado beyond reach of judge and jury.

This vine produces annually from 8,000 to 10,000 pounds of grapes. Its product is said to have reached occasionally 14,000 pounds. The extension of the vine is limited only by the trellis supporting it, the branches being an inch or two in diameter where they are cut off at the edge. A smaller vine near by is about fourteen years old, and gives promise of becoming a rival except that it is hemmed in between the larger vine and a house. They certainly prove the wonderful adaptability of the soil and climate to vine culture.

Hyatt's "Hand Book of Grape Culture" thus begins a chapter on this vine: "We call this the Mammoth, not so much on account of the size of its fruit as of the vine itself and of its prodigious prolific properties. It is one of the celebrities of Southern California. It was the riding whip of a Spanish woman, given by her lover, which she planted," (not the lover but the whip) "and it has developed into that grand memento of love, the largest and most famous vine in the world."

COL. HOLLISTER'S.

The following description of the grounds and farm of this well-known gentleman, is taken from recent correspondence of the New York *World:*

"While at Santa Barbara I visited a representative

or model farm. An account of the visit will convey a better idea of the resources of the country than any general description. We drove up the beautiful valley a dozen miles, to where a wide opening of the coast hills gave an extended view of the sea. Here we entered a well-made avenue at the side of a grove of magnificent live-oaks leading to the residence, visible miles away, of Col. Hollister, one of the great wool growers of this region. The house was imbedded in a mass of roses, carnations, verbenas, geraniums, calla lilies, fuchsias, gladioli, and other rare flowers, while its interior indicated the culture and taste of its occupants.

We were cordially greeted by Col. Hollister, the millionaire of Santa Barbara county, whose frank hospitality made us perfectly at home. * * * * Re-entering our carriage we drove over an excellent road skirted by live-oaks, through gates opening and closing to the touch of the carriage wheels, winding round the edge of valleys, crossing gullies, and cutting through the crests of little hills; past fields of wheat, barley and corn, and great orchards of growing almond and walnut trees, till we reached a beautiful level plain hidden close away under the mountain, at the head of which the new and ample summer cottage stands. Here also we enjoyed a beautiful ocean view, and unsurpassed nearer visions of sloping hillside and rugged mountain, with their many varied tints of green. A further drive of a mile up the valley—for though we were apparently close under the mountain, the cañon opened fertile and inviting far away on either side—

brought us to one of Mr. H.'s tea plantations. He has imported not only the plants but experienced laborers, and remarked that he was trying the plant in every possible situation as to soil and exposure, that he might determine to which it is best adapted.

A genuine Central Park omnibus stands in the carriage house, for transporting the family to and fro between the winter and summer residences. The winding roads wrought out of the hillside, the groves of forest trees, valley and glen and rocky mountain side found their counterpart in my memory only in that gem of Llewellyn Park, at Orange, N. J., and it seemed to me the proprietors must be kindred spirits.

Col. H. showed me sample stalks of wheat ripening, six and seven feet high, with heads of proportionate size, and a bunch of barley numbering 170 stalks, the product of a single seed! His fields were luxuriant with the burr clover and alfileria, the rich annual grass of this region. The excellence of these grasses can hardly be understood by the eastern reader. The burrs are very full of nutriment, and equally good when dry.

Col. H. has an orchard of 7,000 almond trees, and will transplant 30,000 more this year. I saw here tomato plants of three years' growth in blossom, and ripening fruit on the same vine ; also crisp and tender celery, growing rank, three feet above ground. It was in no way inferior, only different in color, to the finest that ever graced Delmonico's. Here were the beautiful acacias, a flowering tree, only two years old, six inches in diameter, and near by I saw almond trees of luxuriant growth, and in full bearing, only three years old.

Col. H. has on his ranchos up the coast over 50,000 sheep, and I saw an elegant hunting-horn, manufactured from the horn of the buck Grizzly, from whose back, in 1859, was taken a fleece of fourteen months and ten days' growth, weighing forty-two and a half pounds!

Without taking this as a criterion, I could credit the remark of our host, that here one enjoyed not only a perfect climate, but tilled the soil with the least labor and for the largest returns of any portion of our country. Land here is not abundant in market. Large tracts can occasionally be bought at $10 an acre. As divided it will bring much more. As I left this inviting spot I ventured to predict that ten years hence the Santa Barbara valley for sixty miles along the bay will by reason of its unsurpassed climate and fertile soil, have become a very garden, in which this beautiful farm will stand prominent as the gem of Southern California, an example of what beneficent Nature and the skilled hand of one of her worshippers can do towards creating an earthly paradise."

CLIMATE.

No general remarks can be made concerning the climate of California. Nothing can be said of it that is not true of one section and false as to another. The *wind* is the all-important element of comfort or discomfort, of use or destruction, on this coast. North of Point Concepcion the coast during the summer is swept by cold fog-bearing winds from the northwest, and by violent rain storms from the south during the winter. Below this Point the whole coast has a very different climate, being both warmer and dryer, but this valley is peculiarly sheltered otherwise. The county has the only coast line facing southward on the Pacific coast between Alaska and Guatamala; the Santa Ynez range of mountains, 4,000 feet high, traverses it from east to west. These peculiar features of its topography greatly affect its climate. Extending eastward for one hundred miles along the sea shore south of these mountains, is a belt of land from three to six miles in width, the climate of which is almost tropical, and unsurpassed by that of any other part of the world. Snow rarely falls on the highest peaks—frost is almost unknown—and it seldom rains from April to December. The mountains behind shut off the northwest trades, and the mountainous islands in front arrest the rain-bearing winds of winter. These, with its position by the sea, produce its wonderful evenness of temperature through all the months. The sea between the islands and the shore is almost as smooth as a river. Old sea captains assert that the only part of the coast fit for a residence is that below Point Concepcion.

There are essentially two climates in California—the land and the sea climate. The latter derives its low and even temperature from the ocean, which along the coast stands at 52° to 54° through the year. The summers are hotter in the north. One might travel from Santa Barbara northward in summer for 300 miles, and find it hotter everywhere than here, or go southeast the same distance to Fort Yuma, one of the hottest places in the world.

In speaking of the "rainy season" we do not mean a season of constant rains, or anything like it. The term is employed only in contrast with the dry season and implies the possibility of rain rather than its actual occurrence. In this county, even in the seasons of most rain by far the larger part of the winter is bright and clear weather. It is usually regarded as the most pleasant part of the year. It is spring rather than winter, and most of the rain falls at night. The grass starts as soon as the soil is wet, and at Christmas the land is covered with green.

The climate is always kindly. We are not troubled by the hot, exhausting days of the Eastern summer, which have no respite at night. In portions of the county the air is so dry and pure that fresh meat dries up instead of spoiling. Cloudy days seldom occur. Frost never reaches across the valley to the foothills. We have no thunder-storms, and the showers must needs be short and gentle that aggregate only twelve inches a year. From April to December there is no rain and one day is as another—bright, beautiful and life-giving. The gentle sea breeze is tonic and invigorating, and relieves the climate from enervation. The days combine the freshness of early spring in the Atlantic states with the softness and dreaminess of the Indian summer, and every day is a new delight. If one thinks of this continuing all the year with hardly twenty days' exception, he cannot doubt that Santa Barbara has a climate as nearly perfect as can be found. Nowhere else is the actual pleasure of mere existence so sensibly experienced as here.

Climate for Invalids.

It is conceded by all visitors to be beneficial, not only for pulmonary complaints, but for a large class of other diseases. Fever and ague is unheard of. Rheumatism and kindred troubles find a specific in the mineral waters of the Hot Springs. Invalids make slight, if any, changes in amount of clothing through the year. Outdoor life is never repellent and never impracticable. Professor Bennett, of the University of Edinburg, writes concerning phthisis: "Much has been written of climate, but the one which appears to be best is that which will enable the patient to pass a few hours every day in the open air without exposure to cold or vicissitudes of temperature on the one hand, or extreme heat on the other." He could not have described the climate of Santa Barbara more accurately.

On this topic we have ample testimony of medical men, from which we will quote sparingly, as being authoritative.

A report was recently made to the State Medical Society by Dr. M. H. Biggs, from which we extract as follows:

"I beg to make a few remarks in regard to the climate of that portion of the county of Santa Barbara which consists of a narrow strip of land lying on the coast, beginning at Point Concepcion and ending at Point San Buenaventura. About two-thirds of it is undulating or rolling land, the rest is in level spots, and all of the richest soil. Santa Barbara is blessed with an exceptional climate; its equal not being on the Pacific coast, at least not outside of the tropics. * * * It is considered exceedingly warm should the thermometer rise to seventy-eight or eighty degrees at noon, and it hardly ever exceeds this unless caused by fires in the neighboring mountains, which now and then occur during the fall of the year.

"The most remarkable fact in regard to this region is the seeming impossibility for epidemics to visit it. The small-pox has ravaged the whole country three or four times since 1843. It has been singularly virulent in San Luis Obispo, the first town north of us, and also in Los Angeles, which lies in the next county south. During the prevalence of the epidemic persons have come from these neighboring towns with the seeds of the disease, and have died in Santa Barbara within a few days of arriving, but some antiseptic property in the climate has prevented the contagion, and it has never spread. Scarlatina and diphtheria are unknown here. There are some instances of the measles having been brought here, but it has never spread as an epidemic. There are no malarious fevers. Persons who come here, afflicted with fever and ague, rarely have more than two or three attacks. They soon become well, even without the use of antiperiodics. The climate seems sufficient to cure the malady. During a residence of twenty years, I have seen only one case of membranous croup, and heard of two others. There is no disease endemic to Santa Barbara.

"Many consumptives visit this part of the country and derive much benefit from its equable climate, which makes it especially appropriate to this class of patients, who besides find much attraction in the pleasant drives along the hard sea beach, or in the healthful rides and walks up the many romantic little dells and valleys and over the low rolling hills, covered here and there with clumps of evergreen oak, sycamore, cotton-wood laurel, alder, and other trees and shrubs too numerous to mention. We have every attraction that one of these days will make Santa Barbara a favorite resort for invalids, convalescents, and all those who desire to pass a quiet, peaceful and healthy life."

Dr. Thomas M. Logan, of Sacramento, President of the United States Medical Association, made a visit to Santa Barbara as Secretary of the California State Board of Health, in pursuit of a suitable place for a State Sanitarium, and reported to the Legislature, giving this place the preference over all others. In a letter to the San Francisco *Scientific Press*, written from here, he says:

"EDITOR PRESS:—I propose to give the public

through your columns some account of the climate, topography and surroundings of this interesting region, from a sanitary point of view. This portion of California stands out preëminently the land of promise to the weary and desponding invalid.

"Its very conformation and topography, while it explains the cause, speaks to the intelligent reader of a climate that cannot be otherwise than even, mild and soft, and at the same time invigorating with the moist but refreshing sea breezes which the thirsty land sucks in. In vain heretofore since my appointment as Health Officer to the state, have I sought for such a combination of sanitary qualities. Here in this mountain and island-locked valley, rising but a few feet from the waters of the Pacific, all the prerequisites of health are to be found in measures so profuse that I would be accused of poetic extravagance were they duly portrayed. The instrumental and numerical proofs must be left to sustain all I have advanced; but before stating these, which I can now only do in part, (reserving the fuller details for a state report,) I proceed to speak more particularly of the town proper, which furnishes the type of the whole region reviewed, and where the statistical and meteorogical data have been carefully compiled by trustworthy observers.

* * * * * *

"In fact nothing can now check the march of improvement which in the last three years has advanced in a geometrical ratio, going on at the same rate towards building up this, the promised land, into a health resort, unsurpassed in artificial, as it is in natural, advantages by any place on the coast, the continent or the world.

"Were I writing from any other than a sanitary standpoint, I could dwell on the refined and cultivated society to be here met with. I could also speak of gardens redolent with the perfume of every kind of flower, of tasteful cottages, and of landscape views, which for loveliness and variety are rarely equaled. These meet one at every turn, and almost tempt me while I write to stray into paths of descriptive romance. But I have taken up my pen to speak of facts—of climate and of vital statistics—and to those I must confine myself.

"About four miles from town, picturesquely located in one of the cañons of the mountains, are hot sulphur springs, which have become favorably known as a place of resort for invalids, especially those suffering from rheumatic affections.

"I learn from good authority that while the country was subject to the crown of Spain, the government sent out a commission of qualified scientific observers to make an examination and analysis of all mineral waters, both in Mexico and upon the Pacific coast, and that this commission, after spending much time prosecuting their inquiries, reported the most favorably on the properties of these springs.

"There is no day in the year in which the invalid may not sit out of doors. This covers the most essential indication in the treatment of consumption, by affording a continuous supply of pure air for the lungs. Still, as the climate possesses some latent peculiarities in its favor, too subtile for ordinary observation, I shall instance the remarkable phenomenon so philosophically noted by Dr. Brinkerhoff, who has resided here eighteen years:

" ' Some ten miles from Santa Barbara, in the bed of the ocean, about one and a half miles from the shore, is an immense spring of petroleum, the product of which continually rises to the surface and floats upon it over an area of many miles. This mineral oil may be seen any day from the deck of the steamers plying between here and San Francisco, or from the high banks along the shore. Having read statements that during the past few years the authorities of Damascus and other plague-ridden cities of the East have resorted to the practice of introducing crude petroleum into the gutters of the streets to disinfect the air, and as a preventive of disease, which practice has been attempted with the most favorable results, I throw out the suggestion whether the prevailing sea breezes, passing over this wide expanse of petroleum, may not take up and bear along some subtile power which serves as a disinfecting agent, and which may account for the infrequency of some of the diseases referred to, and possibly for the superior healthfulness of the climate of Santa Barbara.'

" I would add that my attention has been directed to the peculiar ambrosial influence pervading the air, described above, and that I endorse all that has been stated in this respect. That the climate of Santa Barbara possesses all the elements of general healthfulness in an eminent degree, is substantiated by the fact that the epidemics incident to childhood are almost unknown. Fevers and agues never originate here. Small-pox, frequently brought from abroad, never spreads, although hundreds of the native population, either from ignorance or prejudice, never allow themselves to be vaccinated.

"The following statistics of the town and county of Santa Barbara are taken from the United States census returns for this county for the year ending June 1, 1870, and speak more for the healthfulness of the place than anything I can add :

"'Population of the town, 2,970. Number of births, 131; deaths of children under one year of age, 9; ratio of births to deaths, $14\frac{1}{2}$ to 1. Total number of deaths, including adults for the same period, 23; ratio of deaths to the whole population, 1 in 130, or .77 of 1 per cent.

"'Population of the county, 7,987. Number of births, same period, 235; total number of deaths of children under one year of age, 15; ratio of births to deaths, $15\frac{3}{4}$ to one, or nearly 16 to 1. Total number of deaths in the county, 64, two accidental; percentage of deaths to total population, 1 to 125, or .80 of 1 per cent.'

"A comparison will enable the reader to form a more distinct idea of the smallness of this death ratio. In San Francisco the annual deaths per 1,000 are 21.4;

in Sacramento, 24 ; in Boston, 24 ; in Chicago, 24.5 ; in New York, 29.8 ; in Santa Barbara, 8.

One of our leading physicians, Dr. S. B. Brinkerhoff, who has resided here some eighteen years, has prepared the following statement of his experience and observation :

"I think I am prepared to speak advisedly of the superiority of the climate of Santa Barbara, and of the very favorable advantages which this place affords as a resort for invalids.

" To the peculiar location and surroundings of Santa Barbara I attribute, mainly, its superior healthfulness. The softness and general uniformity of the climate, its freedom from dampness and sudden changes, the opportunity for diversion and recreation, render Santa Barbara preëminently a desirable place of resort for persons suffering from bronchial and pulmonary affections. Although many persons suffering from these complaints have come here too late to receive any permanent relief from the restorative effects of the climate, yet the greater portion of cases which have come under my observation have been permanently relieved, and many in a surprisingly short space of time have been perfectly restored to health. That the climate of Santa Barbara possesses elements of general healthfulness in an eminent degree, and perhaps, also, some latent peculiarities in its favor too subtile for ordinary observation, I may instance the following facts in this connection : During the eighteen years of my active practice here, I have never known a single case of scarlet fever or diphtheria. I have known of only three cases of dysentery, neither of which proved fatal; and of only three cases of membranous croup. The epidemics and diseases incident to childhood, which in other parts of the country sweep away thousands of children annually, are here comparatively unknown. Cases of fever and ague I have never known originating here, and persons coming here afflicted with it, rarely have more than two or three attacks, even without the use of anti-periodics. I have known instances of small-pox at three different times. In each of the first two instances, occurring several years apart, the disease was confined to a single case, and was contracted elsewhere. Neither of these cases proved fatal. In the year 1864, when this disease prevailed so extensively, and proved so fatal throughout the state, there were two cases of disease contracted elsewhere and developed here, both of which proved fatal. Three other persons residing here contracted the disease from contagion at this time, all of whom recovered. Although no unusual precaution was taken to prevent the spread of the disease, it was confined to the cases mentioned. In the years 1869-70, when this disease, in its most virulent form prevailed so generally throughout the state, not a single case occurred at Santa Barbara, although in daily communication with other parts of the state by stage and steamer.

"The hot springs are favorably known as a resort for certain classes of invalids. I do not regard the use of these waters by any means as a panacea for all ' the ills which flesh is heir to,' but for the cure of certain diseases they are unmistakably efficacious. I have known some cases which seemed to defy all powers of medication, cured permanently, in a surprisingly short time by the water of these springs advisedly used as a beverage and for bathing. The indiscriminate use of them may be disadvantageous, and even positively injurious, and before resorting to them, patients should always consult some physician as to their proper use.

"Some invalids will find it desirable to select their residence while here, where they can enjoy the advantages of sea bathing. In some cases they derive more benefit by seeking a higher altitude, which can easily be obtained within a short distance of the town, where comfortable accomodations can be secured. The matters of pleasant location, diet, exercise and recreation are all-important to the invalid, and upon a proper regulation and observance of the same, as well as the influences of a favorable climate, may greatly depend his speedy recovery."

"Of the thousands who have this season come to California for the sake of its climate, some hundreds, under the guidance of a lucky star, are here in this valley of beauty, this haven of rest.

"We who have spent some time here in Santa Barbara can say—knowing whereof we speak—that California does afford a most desirable climate; and many who come here almost prostrate with disease now pre sent that most convincing testimonial—a strong physique, the firm, quick step and ruddy cheek.

"I have felt much interest in comparing the climate of this valley with that of Florida, so much sought by invalids. So far as I have been able to compare month with month, the range of the thermometer here very nearly coincides with that of St. Augustine or Pilatka, Florida; but there is this essential difference to note: while the climate of Florida is peculiarly wanting in that subtile, tonic property which gives one vim and vivacity, that of California is remarkable for the presence of that quality. To describe each in a word— the former is enervating, the latter bracing.

"In point of scenery and general attractiveness, the difference between the two countries is too great to admit of comparison. In place of monotonous prose there, we find here the most sparkling poetry of nature; in lieu of sand flats, we are here greeted by rich valleys and vine clad hills, with a luxuriance of vegetation and a wealth of flowers and foliage which must put to everlasting shame Ponce de Leon's land, even with its flowery name and tropical pretensions.

"This much of comparing and contrasting for the benefit of those of your readers who are still adrift in quest of the best climate, the most inviting places. During the last two years I have had occasion either to visit or otherwise inform myself of health resorts, both in Europe and in the various quarters of our own country, and I have to say that over all of which I have knowledge, the palm belongs to Santa Barbara, California. Nowhere else have we seen nature so lavish of her best gifts, so profuse in her bestowment of all that is good. Not only does she give us the best of air to breathe, the most thoroughly tempered breezes, the nearest approximation to freedom from change of temperature and from local diseases, and to soil producing all the grains and fruits and flowers of our continent; but there is superadded for our esthetic enjoyment one of nature's choicest picture galleries, the walls hung with some of the most pleasing productions of her own inimitable hand. And now at Christmas time, while in accordance with a custom that should never die, ten thousand fair hands are busied entwining evergreens and wreathing flowers for church and home, this Queen of Artists has freshened and adorned her gallery here as if especially for the festive days in honor of her author. As we feast our eyes upon the hills around us here all clothed in the freshest and richest of green, and breathe in the plenteous perfume which fills street and common, no small measure of imagination is needed to realize fairly that our homes, not only those far up the New England coast, or on the shores of the great lakes, but those on the borders of the 'Sunny South,' as well, are locked in ice or covered with snow. Did not the telegraph and mail bring the story to us, surely we should never dream it here."—*Correspondence of the Cincinnati Gazette.*

"San Francisco, March 10, 1872.
"A friend and neighbor of my own, consumptive

for some years, and struggling for his life in a winter residence for some two years at Nice and Mentone, and a third year at Aiken, came last October to Southern California. He had been 'losing ground,' as he said, and as his appearance showed, for two years, and last summer suffered so severely from night sweats, sleeplessness, continual coughing and lack of appetite, that it was doubtful whether he would live through the winter anywhere; and it was rather in desperation than with much hope of a prolonged or comfortable life, that he made ready for the journey across the continent with his family. In January I was standing in the doorway of a hotel at Los Angeles, when I saw a wagon drive up; the driver jumped out, held out his hand to me, and sung out in a hearty voice, 'How do you do?' It was my consumptive friend, but a changed man. He had just driven sixty miles in two days, over a rough road, from San Buenaventura; he walked with me several miles on the evening we met; he ate heartily and slept well, enjoyed his life and coughed hardly at all. It was an amazing change to come about in three months, and in a man so far gone in consumption as he was.

"I think I shall be doing a service therefore to many invalids, if I give you here some details concerning these places, but little known as yet in the East, which are now so accessible, and whose beneficial influences upon diseases of the throat and lungs are undoubtedly remarkable.

"San Diego, Santa Barbara and San Bernardino are

the three points most favorable for consumptives and persons subject to throat difficulties.

"Santa Barbara is on many accounts the pleasantest of all the three places I have named; and it has an advantage in this that one may there choose his climate, within a distance of three or four miles of the town. It has a very peculiar situation. * * * The town and its vicinity have thus a remarkably equal climate. I have before me a number of reports of temperature and could overwhelm you if I liked with figures, tables and statistics concerning the whole coast; but these records are almost altogether of mean temperature for a week, month or year. Now what an invalid suffers most from is not recorded in such tables; I mean the daily extremes. If the day is very warm and the evening suddenly chilly and cold, that makes a bad climate for weakly persons. Now both Santa Barbara and San Diego are remarkably free from such sudden and great changes, and I think there is no doubt that Santa Barbara has the most equable climate, in this sense as well as all others, on this coast.

"Persons who come to California for the winter should bring their winter clothing. You do not need a shawl or an overcoat if you are exercising, but in driving they are necessary. You can sit out of doors almost every day, either to read or write, or in any other occupation, for there are but few rainy days, and it no sooner stops raining than the sun shines out most brilliantly and kindly. I do not think there were five days in Santa Barbara in December, January and

February, in which the tenderest invalid could not pass the greater part of the day out of doors with pleasure and benefit. But in the evening you will sit by a wood fire—mostly with the doors and windows open—and at night you sleep under blankets very comfortably. The constant or almost uninterrupted brightness of the skies has, I suspect, a good deal to do with the healthful influences of the climate. The Southern counties have but little rain. There are no gloomy days. Occasionally there is a fog in the morning, but it is not a cold fog—rather dry and warm, like the Newport fogs.

"Living at the hotels is very reasonable—from $10 to $14 per week; fires are an extra charge, but you should secure a room with a fire place or stove. Horses can be bought in Santa Barbara for from $20 to $50; and for children there are donkeys for which you pay from $5 to $10. You find at all of the hotels good beds, and plain but sufficient and various food. Santa Barbara has the advantages of pleasant society and excellent schools. It is, in fact, a cozy nest of New England and Western New York people, many of whom originally came here for their health, and remain because they are charmed with the climate. It has a number of pleasant drives, and the old Spanish part of the town is an agreeable novelty to strangers.

"We do not expect to find in Southern California yet, artistically finished pleasure resorts. Such as they are, however, the places I have named

deserve the visit of persons suffering from throat or lung disease, and it will be no small addition to their merits that they can be reached without a voyage across the Atlantic, and that they present for the amusement of the visitor many novel and curious phases of life."
—*Charles Nordhoff in New York Tribune.*

TEMPERATURE.

This is a matter of all-important interest to the sufferer from lung troubles. To say a place has a mean annual temperature of 51° like New York, or 60° like Santa Barbara, proves nothing whatever to the healthful evenness of the climate. Nor does it help matters very much to give monthly means, showing that New York oscillates between 30°, the mean of February, and 73°, that of July, while Santa Barbara averages 55° and 68° for the same months, as was the case last year. At the East a variation of 30° or 40° between two consecutive days, or even during the same day, is by no means uncommon,—here it is unheard of. In order to fully test a climate the temperature must be known for every day of the year and compared with the enormous diurnal variations of some familiar place, such as New York city. In view of the *great* importance of this exhibit to intelligent physicians and a large class of invalids, we have compiled the following table, showing the temperature of every day from July 1, 1871, to June 30, 1872, inclusive, as taken from three daily readings of the thermometer in this town:

	July.	Aug.	Sept.	Oct.	Nov.	Dec.	Jan.	Feb.	M'ch	April	May.	June
1.....	63	69	67	71	70	49	54	56	53	57	60	58
2.....	65	68	67	83 *	61	52	49	55	59	57	63	65
3.....	66	68	68	77 *	57	52	50	58	59	60	61	65
4.....	67	68	71	69	58	55	51	59	58	55	61	64
5.....	67	67	69	65	55	54	52	55	57	58	66	73
6.....	67	66	70	63	55	58	53	59	58	54	60	68
7.....	65	70	66	65	53	51	53	53	61	53	66	62
8.....	68	68	66	61	56	51	54	54	61	56	67	64
9.....	66	69	66	61	56	55	53	61	60	54	63	65
10.....	67	69	66	63	58	53	48	60	62	58	59	64
11.....	68	68	70	65	52	53	50	58	60	55	61	63
12.....	67	68	66	61	55	55	50	52	63	59	62	67
13.....	70	67	67	62	55	58	53	55	54	53	61	67
14.....	73	66	66	66	50	57	55	55	54	58	57	67
15.....	72	70	65	59	57	56	53	52	60	58	62	63
16.....	71	72	64	69	59	55	53	55	58	56	61	65
17.....	70	78 *	61	71	61	55	52	57	64	53	60	63
18.....	67	79 *	62	71	55	56	52	61	57	52	67	67
19.....	67	75 *	65	64	59	56	52	60	52	58	62	74 *
20.....	71	70	70	62	60	58	56	59	55	58	61	80 *
21.....	73	70	64	62	59	54	57	55	57	64	59	82 *
22.....	74	70	65	65	63	52	54	54	56	62	59	87 *
23.....	73	72	66	63	59	53	54	52	54	63	61	78 *
24.....	72	72	62	59	62	57	48	50	54	59	63	69
25.....	67	68	61	61	61	56	43	51	56	61	65	67
26.....	64	67	61	62	57	53	44	51	58	61	65	68
27.....	69	67	62	61	55	54	47	49	59	62	65	71
28.....	72	66	63	63	54	57	51	52	58	61	64	67
29.....	69	69	61	60	52	56	49	50	56	62	65	69
30.....	68	69	62	58	48	54	52	...	55	60	67	74
31.....	70	68	...	61	...	55	52	...	54	...	63	...
	68.5	69.5	65.3	64.6	56.7	54.5	51.5	55.1	57.5	57.9	62.5	68.5

The lower line shows the mean of each month. The mean of the entire year is 61°. On the days marked with an asterisk the thermometer was abnormally high on account of mountain fires back of the town.

Warmest day of the year, June 22..87°
Warmest days, except for mountain fires, July 22, 1871, and

June 30, 1872..74°
Coldest day of the year, January 25..43°

Divided into seasons as in the Atlantic states the temperature of the last two years, during which records have been kept, was as follows:

	1870-1.	1871-2.
Mean of spring	59.8°	59.3°
Mean of summer	68.7°	68.8°
Mean of autumn	65°	62.2°
Mean of winter	53.3°	53.7°
Yearly mean	61.2°	61°

It will be observed that, taking one year with another, the thermometrical range is almost identical.

SCENERY.

The main road approaching Santa Barbara from the north, crossing the Santa Ynez mountains, is very romantic. It winds up steep mountains by zig-zags and crosses sandy creeks and marshy valleys until it reaches the Gaviota pass—a natural chasm about sixty feet wide through the lofty range reaching within a mile of the sea. The sides of this pass are nearly perpendicular walls of solid rock. From the pass the road winds at the base of these mountains for nearly twenty miles along the sea beach. It is a delightful trip in the summer—the white crested billows of the Pacific curling and seething about the horses' feet; and the cool sea breeze, how refreshing—after leaving the hot and dusty roads over the mountains.

After passing the immense estate of Dos Pueblos the

traveler rides for miles through a fine rural settlement of small farms, with neat little painted dwellings surrounded by orange, lemon, almond, walnut, fig and other fruit and shade trees, with well kept front yards filled with shrubs, vines, flowers, lawns and other tasteful adornments. In the centre of this cheerful line of pleasant houses stands a neat and comfortable school house with green blinds, showing the right sort of spirit in the people who are settling the country.

Every kind of scenery may be found here, from the level plain to the inaccessible peak ; cultivated farms, red-wood forests and dreary wastes ; little valleys sunk into the earth, down into which one looks from the broader level, as into another world ; where the giant sycamores twist themselves toward the upper air, and lithe limbed deer browse in the cool shadows.

Running brooks and green summer fields we cannot have ; but in the rainy season six months of brilliant green covers the whole face of nature from sea to mountain top. Instead of the snows and frozen ground of the Atlantic states the eye is charmed with the most inviting of pictures. A correspondent of the New York *Evening Mail* writes as follows : " The hills at this season are carpeted with the richest green ; the mountains loom up grandly with ever changing shadows, the clear atmosphere marking distinctly their outline against the blue of the heavens over them ; the air is fragrant with the perfume of flowers and blossoming fruit trees. Old Ocean beats tirelessly against the shore with a gentle, peaceful melody. The waters of the Pacific stretch far and wide, blue under a cloudless sky, the faint outline of islands rising from them. Here are fine mountain and ocean scenery—always a rare combination—bathing, boating, fishing, hunting and driving, no shivering from cold, no depressing heat. fruits, flowers, with the purest air and the brightest sunshine." A writer in the San Jose *Mercury* thus refers to the view from the old Mission: "We paused, as we stood once more on the steps outside, struck with the beauty of the picture which spread out like a dream before us. The gentle slope to the town; then the white and various colored houses nestled down in their embracing trees; farther, the sparkling waters of the ocean, blue and languid in the sunlight, while far out toward the horizon's verge were the Santa Barbara Islands, lying misty and dim between the sea and sky. On our right, the country with its hills and trees and foliage; on our left, the bold, rugged mountains of the Santa Barbara range. What a lovely picture! beyond the power of pen to describe. We rode slowly back to our hotel, filled with its glory."

Fishing and Hunting.

Game of various kinds abounds in the county. The famous grizzly may be met in the mountains, if any one desires such an interview. Such meetings are not apt to be wholly satisfactory except to the grizzly, as he usually closes the proceedings by eating the interviewer. Hare are numerous, where the sage bush grows to afford them shelter. Rabbits are found everywhere. Wild ducks are abundant in the winter, on the miniature ponds in the fields, caused by the rains. Quail are plentiful in the foot hills. There are many of the small brown or "cinnamon" bear in the mountains, and also the California lion, a species of panther. Deer may even be seen grazing among the cattle as feed and water grow scarce in the late summer. The mountain streams offer fine trout to disciples of Isaak Walton, and there are as good fish in the sea as ever were caught for those who would angle more luxuriously. The taking of game is regulated by law, which prohibits the killing of deer except between August 1st and January 1st; doves except between September 15th and March 15th; quails except between September 15th and March 15th; ducks except between September 15th and March 15th; trout except between May 1st and October 1st.

IRRIGATION.

Nearly all letters of inquiry ask particularly in regard to irrigation, its uses, expense, etc. In reply we say that irrigation is not necessary in that portion of the county west of the Rincon hill, for any crop except strawberries, and is not practiced here. Below Ventura, farmers irrigate their crops from ditches or canals several miles long, running parallel with the rivers, or from artesian wells. In the western part strawberries and flowers are improved by summer watering, but nothing else—unless it be the streets. Deep plowing and occasional stirring of the soil do more than irrigation; and most of our farmers get large crops without either. Grapes and other fruits have a richer flavor without water.

AGRICULTURE.

Between the Santa Ynez and Santa Susanna ranges, and at their base along the coast, there are a number of exceedingly beautiful and fertile valleys, most of them being more or less under cultivation. Between the Santa Ynez and San Rafael mountains is a broad extent of excellent land, watered by the Santa Ynez river, and available for any of the purposes of farming. This river traverses the county for 100 miles, emptying into the Pacific. The San Buenaventura rises near the centre and flows southward to the sea. The Santa Clara flows westward across the county, having its mouth near Ventura. The Santa Maria is quite a stream and forms the northern boundary of the county for over 100 miles. It sinks into the sand in several places near its mouth. There is but little timber except oak, willow and sycamore, which grow on the plains or in the valleys. The hills are covered with grass or wild oats during the winter and spring, furnishing nutritious pasturage for sheep and cattle through the entire year. In the eastern portions are forests of pine and red-wood. East of Santa Barbara is a nearly level plain averaging two miles in width

and fifteen in length, flanked by fertile foot hills, f
the most part under careful cultivation. Some of the
finest barley raised in the state is produced in these
valleys of Montecito and Carpenteria, and most kinds
of fruit are cultivated. The terrace west of town is
several miles wide and reaches to Point Concepcion.
Saticoy and Santa Clara valleys are in the eastern part
of the county, and have a coast line of sixteen miles,
extending inland about forty miles ; they also are very
fertile. These valleys produce immense quantities of
wild mustard ; wild bees are very numerous, and yield
a good deal of honey and wax. The silk worm thrives
here finely. Almost everywhere water is obtained at
moderate depth, and wind mills can be employed if desired. This suffices for the family, the cattle and the
gardens of the farmer; his grain crops do not want
summer water nor his fruit trees. A one-year-old hive
of bees will often produce thirty pounds of liquid honey
and two pounds of clean wax. At no distant time
honey and wax will become part of our exports.

The cañons are peculiar, often running up into the
mountains, and branching off in unexpected directions,
opening out fertile tracts where only hills were looked
for. This feature gives a greater extent of available
land than is at first apparent; and here, as everywhere
else, it becomes one not to be deceived by first appearances, since here no one is safe from a great surprise.

Much of our roughest land will in time become the
most valuable, as it is being demonstrated that the
hills are the best adapted to grape culture, and scarcely

any hill is too precipitous for growing vines. Most of the arable land is gently rolling. C. L. Brace, in the *New West*, says: "In a material point of view the sunny and fertile region about Santa Barbara is undoubtedly the most desirable part of the state for an immigrant; that is, land in proportion to its cost will yield more to the cultivator." There is an opening to immigration now from the fact that several of the large estates are being broken up. Sheep raising can be carried on here to great profit. But the great wealth of the region must always lie in its fruits, and whatever of these can be condensed or preserved for market will always pay. In the Santa Clara valley are several large ranches belonging to Thos. A. Scott, of Philadelphia, aggregating a quarter million acres now offered for sale in small farms. The coast and valley portions of the entire county are destined to be divided into small tracts suitable for orchard, vineyard or tillage, and to pass into the hands of wine or fruit growers. If these are enterprising Eastern men or thrifty Germans their reward will be both sure and abundant.

The country is best of all adapted for men of small capital, who are farmers or vine growers. For such it offers great inducements. When you buy a farm you buy clear land. For ten months out of twelve the new settler can camp in a tent; he need be in no haste to build barns; he has no forest to clear; he has only to fence his ground and begin plowing. Feed is ready for his stock on all the hills. His land, which costs anywhere from $2 to $25 an acre, at once begins to rise in value with cultivation. All the luxuries of farm life he can have speedily. In three years he can enjoy a variety of fruits from his own orchards, and his vegetables are such as are seen nowhere else in the world. He can get good stock cheap and raise it easily. He may try sheep raising on the brown hills, or keep a dairy rancho, or breed fowls for market, or raise hops, or flax, or the castor bean, or almost any fruit or cereal. No cultivator in the world has so many different products to turn to.

As soon as the first rains of December have moistened the soil every plow is set to work. The planting season is long, extending to April, during which time rain does not interfere with work more than during the summer at the East. Wheat and barley are commonly sown for hay and cut before the heads fill. Farmers are not obliged to work hard half the summer to provide food for carrying their stock over the winter; they save three-fourths of the expense of fuel needed at the East; they have no cattle stables to clean; the absence of winter lightens the work and exposure of women; vegetables may be had fresh from the garden most or all of the year; fruit is plenty and cheap. Fowls pick up their living at all times. Tree growth is very rapid and has slight interruption in winter. Trees grow as much in four years as in the Atlantic states in eight. Flowers will grow about the house continually. The wages of farm hands are $20 to $30 a month the year round, or $30 to $40 in harvest, with board and lodging. Wheat, oats and barley are threshed on the field, and left there till wanted. Potatoes stay in the ground long after ripening without harm. Thus the farmer saves the expense of large barns and the carrying of his crops to and fro. He is not hurried by short seasons or fear of rain, and he needs fewer hands. His wheat is dry and glutinous, keeping sweet long, and making the best flour in the world. Nor does he need to put away much food for his cattle. A quarter acre of beets, replanted as used, supports a cow through the year. Work horses have barley and hay, but sheep are never fed ; market cattle fatten in the pastures and horses not at work pick up their living on the commons, both in winter and summer. The alfalfa does well for pigs, cows, and even plow horses, and bears enormous crops. It yields from six to eight cuttings a year. The soil gives a much greater product here than in older states. The farmer often takes fifty, sixty, even eighty bushels of wheat from an acre, and sometimes forty bushels of " volunteer " where he has not sown, and can even gather forty bushels of volunteer barley for three years without sowing or cultivating.

"One cannot help noticing that the forms of the women who have been here long are more full and robust than with us, while the children are universally chubby, fat and red-cheeked. I do not remember seeing a single weakly child. All animals also fatten easily here. Most of the country is so fit for a garden that it is wasteful to use it for a cattle or sheep range, or for field crops. The careful culture of small tracts will pay extraordinary profits. In fact I do not know a country better adapted to farming as we understand the word at the East. The seasons are such as to play into the farmer's hands; the soil is rich and easily worked, and everything grows marvelously. The eucalyptus (an Australian evergreen) has made twenty feet in a year (I have seen one eight years old which was seventy-five feet high and two and a-half feet in diameter at the base). I spent the 22d of February at a pic-nic on one of these oak-covered plains, green as our finest pasture in June, with a lovely lake in the centre of a fair, smooth field, with skies so bright and air so soft that a baby slept on the ground. It had rained hard over night, but we sat on the ground to eat our luncheon."—*Chas. Nordhoff in Harper's Magazine.*

The practical farmer can commence operations assured that a few years spent as industriously as is necessary in farming elsewhere, will have surrounded him with all the necessaries and many of the luxuries of life, make him secure from want, and the owner of a farm, orchard and garden that will afford him and his family a competency, and a comfortable inheritance to his children. Society is changing. Agriculture is assuming its proper position, and all things have a more settled air. The country grows more attractive. The marvelous natural resources of the coast are becoming apparent, and the richness and bounty of its climate and soil are gaining due appreciation.

"Nothing but the ignorance which prevails in our Eastern states of this great treasure in our own territory, could have kept a populous immigration, ere this, from settling and cultivating these favored valleys and hillsides."—*The New West, by C. L. Brace.*

Cheap House Building.

Most houses are of wood, and of the kind called "Balloon" or "Chicago" frames, fastened together with nails and with no upright posts larger than 2x4 inches. These are the strongest kind of wooden buildings. For the farmer in haste to build and to build cheaply, an adobe house is by no means to be despised. It can be built by natives working at $20 a month, of common earth, saving the price of lumber, skilled labor and transportation. The walls are two to three feet thick and the house is very comfortable, being cool in summer and warm in winter. They are roofed with tiles, shingles or "shakes." A comfortable frame house of four rooms and a piazza, for a small family, painted inside and out, and finished with cloth and paper instead of plaster, can be put up in town for $500. On a farm paint, cloth and plaster can be dispensed with for a while, when economy is necessary, and the cost will be much reduced. Dwellings are necessary mainly for privacy, and very slight, cheap structures are as good as the warm and more costly ones of colder climates. As a rule farmers live in small and cheap houses, the climate—which permits children to play out of doors for at least 300 days in the year, and makes the piazza or the neighboring shade tree pleasanter than a room, in winter or summer—being probably to blame for it. The dwelling is a less important part of the farm than at the East. A cellar is not necessary, nor are two stories. A long range of rooms with broad and comfortable piazzas is the best, copied after the adobes of the natives, and very convenient for doing housework. Our fences are cheap, durable and tight. Poles are cut in the chapparal, seven or eight feet long by natives at $8 per 1,000. A plow runs a furrow along the proposed line of fence, the poles are set in the trench close together and tied at a height of five feet to a pole running horizontally, the furrow is filled up with dirt again and the fence is done. The expense is about seventy-five cehts per rod.

Fruit Culture.

In no other part of the world do fruit trees grow so rapidly, bear so early, so regularly and so abundantly, and produce fruit of such large size. Nor is there any other country where so great a variety of fruit can be produced in high excellence. In the matter of flavor our apples, peaches and strawberries are perhaps inferior to Eastern fruit; in the flavor of other species we are at least equal to other countries. The pear, plum, apricot, grape and olive are peculiarly healthy and productive as compared with the same fruits elsewhere. All kinds of fruit trees are trained low. This causes earlier bearing—a matter of importance where the interest on money is so high; the trunk is shaded from too much sun, and the earth about the roots is kept moist. They are free from the curculio. They are as large at two years old as in New York at three or four. Instances of exceptional growth are without parallel. Cherry trees have grown to be fourteen feet high in one year; pear trees ten feet; peach trees to have trunks two to three inches in diameter: all from buds on yearling stocks. They begin to fruit in about half the time required on the Atlantic. The plum is destined to be prominent among fruits. The fig bears in two years from the slip and produces abundantly, two crops a year, and is a large and very handsome shade tree with its dense foliage. The almond and English walnut thrive in perfection in this county, but not much further north; a slight frost destroys the almond. The citron does admirably and bears fruit its fourth year. It will be found exceedingly lucrative. The lime fruits in five years from the seed and has an unlimited market. A peculiar effect of this climate is to cause early and prolific bearing in fruit trees. They often contain more fruit than their trunks can support. Trees an inch and a-half in diameter at the ground, are loaded with large and handsome pears, peaches, etc. Where so little labor brings so large and speedy return, every farmer provides himself with a fruit orchard. Here the buds are not killed by sudden frost, the fruit is not blighted by sharp wind, nor mildewed by dampness, nor bored and destroyed by insects, nor gnarled and twisted by the violent changes and many freaks of a churlish climate.

The trees have twice as much growing time in a year as at the East. Strawberries raised last year in the Montecito valley paid at the rate of $1,200 an acre. Every farmer may have in his grounds peaches, apricots, apples, pears, pomegranates, cherries, figs, quinces, plums, all the berries, melons, cactus fruit, guavas and the palm. Besides these are six fruits—the orange, lemon, almond, citron, olive and English walnut—for which the market extends over the whole United States, while the area in which they can be successfully cultivated is quite limited. The amount of land in the world suitable to these trees is very small, and there is no danger of over supply. Twenty acres cultivated in nut and fruit trees, and in garden, will support a family in comfort if not in affluence.

If there be any one vegetable growth which more than any other finds a congenial home in this region, and which nearly every one plants, it is the grape vine. It grows better on the hillsides than in the valleys and is of fine growth and flavor without irrigation. It stands the long dry summer better than any other plant. The average number of vines to the acre is 600, which produce annually 300 gallons of wine and twenty of brandy from the residuum. In appearance the vine in fruit resembles an umbrella spread out. Stakes are soon dispensed with; the vine acquires great size of stem and supports itself. It bears the second year. A man can plant a vineyard which in six years will bring him in $200 to $400 in wine, or even more in raisins. The ease with which the grape is cultivated its immense yield of fruit, and the readiness with which it can be marketed in different forms, combine to make it a leading branch of industry. Every farm contains a vineyard of greater or less extent. The principal variety now grown is the Mission grape, introduced by the Padres, but the finest foreign varieties do equally well, and are receiving more attention of late. It is on record that one acre in this state has produced fourteen tons of grapes. The cheapest land in the county is proving to be the best for vine culture, namely, the steep hillsides never yet cultivated. Two hundred varieties of grapes are raised in the state. Our vines bear twice as much fruit as elsewhere. The crop never fails. They are grown from cuttings and with little care. All the twigs are cut off yearly, leaving a bare stalk with three or four buds. The vine grown for raisins will be found to pay here five times the profit per acre of wheat, and it is as cheaply cultivated. The process of making raisins is very simple. They are partially dried in the sun and afterwards under cover. The true raisin grape of Malaga has been introduced here and does well. The manufacture of raisins ought to be as profitable as that of wine and far more beneficial to the state.

We close this subject with extracts from a letter of Charles Nordhoff to the New York *Tribune:*

"Santa Barbara county has a long, narrow strip of sea coast, fronting south, which is believed to be peculiarly fitted for the culture of the almond, which in Los Angeles is found to be sometimes hurt by frost.

"The custom is to plant 108 trees to the acre. They begin to bear at three years from the bud; and at five years may be expected to yield twelve pounds to the tree, or say 1,200 pounds per acre, which, at twenty cents per pound, would give $240 per acre. They bear for a number of years; at ten years, I am told, may be counted on for twenty pounds to the tree, which would give $400 to the acre. No disease troubles the tree here, but the squirrel and gopher destroy it when it is young. These however are easily driven out by poison and perseverance; and one man's labor suffices to keep in order twenty or even thirty acres of trees.

"The olive grows slowly at first, begins to bear at four years, under favorable circumstances, but does not yield a full crop until the tenth, or even the twelfth year. It should then return an average of twenty-five gallons of olives per tree. Sixty trees are planted to the acre. The olives are sold here at this time for sixty cents per gallon in the orchard, and the few olive groves now in full bearing about here, at that rate, are worth, gross, $900 per acre per annum. No doubt as new groves come to bear, the price will go down; but there is here an immense margin, as you will perceive. The olives of this state, when carefully pickled, are far superior to those we get from France or Spain. They are of moderate size, but very plump, juicy, and full-flavored. Pickled olives fetch here seventy-five cents per gallon. I am told by proprietors of olive orchards that it is more profitable to make the fruit into oil than to pickle it. From five to seven gallons of ripe olives go to one gallon of oil, and that is worth now $5. The machinery for pressing the oil is very simple. I think there is no finer object than a grove of these healthful, finely-grown trees. There are several young orchards about here, and Santa Barbara is likely to become the centre of this culture. The olive is not particular as to soil, and it does not here need irrigation. The gopher eats the roots of the young tree, but this is its only enemy. That you may not think I have exaggerated the olive tree's productiveness, I will add that one tree in this town, now thirty years old, bore $48 worth of olives for three years in succession; another at twelve years bore over two barrels of olives.

"The English walnut shows itself as a stately, magnificent tree, with clean, grayish bark, and wide-spreading branches. It is, like our own black walnut, a tree of slow growth, and does not begin to bear until it is seven or eight years of age. In twelve years with thorough culture it bears from fifty to seventy-five pounds of nuts; at fifteen years from 100 to 160 pounds; thirty trees may stand on an acre, and it is customary here to plant almond trees between the rows of walnuts, which pay the cost of cultivation and a handsome profit, and are cut down when the walnuts begin to cover the ground. The nuts sold this year for twelve and a half cents per pound, in Los Angeles. A little arithmetic will tell you that at 100 pounds to the tree, which for an orchard fifteen years old would be, everybody tells me, an under estimate, the yield would be $375 per acre. The only expense is the cost of cultivating, and one man could easily care for thirty acres. It is asserted that the tree is absolutely free from disease or enemies in this state; it needs no pruning, and it may be safely transplanted when three years old, so that the planter would get a crop in seven years. At twenty years trees have borne 250 pounds of nuts. Two English walnut trees near Santa Barbara, thirty years old, have yielded $50 worth of nuts each per annum for several years past. The citron, which bears in four or five years, is also a profitable plant. The lemon, which becomes a stately, far-spreading tree, bears in ten years a valuable crop.

"I have found a large number of men of small fortunes, as well as farmers, deliberately giving money and time to the formation of orange, lemon and nut orchards. They say, 'We will work and wait for eight or ten years, in order that at the end we shall have a small fortune, to make our latter years easy;' and if a man may in ten years from twenty acres secure himself a regular income of ten or even five thousand dollars per annum, with but trifling labor and care, these persons would seem to be wise. * * * After a thorough examination I believe Southern California to be the best region in the whole United States for farmers."

WOOL GROWING.

California is probably the best country in the world, except Australia, for raising sheep. Nowhere do they so thrive and multiply with so little care; and no fleeces of similar breeds are so heavy. Here in the mountain pastures they roam and feed themselves the year round. Sheep love length of range, and they have it here; a dry soil and climate is their preference, and in few countries is the dry season so protracted. The cost of keeping sheep is so small and the increase so great that it is a very money-making business. Most of the diseases contracted elsewhere are unknown here. One third of the wool of California is a second crop, clipped in autumn.

The ewes when properly cared for increase a hundred per cent. every year. The cost of keeping large bands is estimated at from thirty-seven to fifty cents per head annually, exclusive of interest on the land used for pasturage. The wool of a good sheep pays twice the cost of keeping; and the wool and lamb together of a fine-blooded ewe are worth eight or ten times the cost.

Cost of Living.

This is probably about the same, or if anything a little less here than at the East. Flour is much cheaper here than in New York; meats half the price or less; clothing about the same; but the high price of labor and the extravagant habits of the people raise all small expenses. The measure of the economy of a people is the subdivision of money. In Germany one gets change to one-tenth of a cent; here the lowest change is the dime or "bit." Books retail at Eastern rates. It costs more to build a house here than one of equal finish at the East because of the higher prices of labor and lumber, the distance from planing mills, etc.

To aid the comparison we append a table from a special report by Edward Young, Chief of Bureau of Statistics, Washington, D. C., showing the average retail prices of provisions, etc., in 1869, in New England and California. To this we have added a column showing present retail prices here:

	Av'ge price in New England, 1869.	Av'ge price in California, 1869.	Av'ge price in Santa Barbara, 1872.
Flour, superfine, per bbl.	$ 9 53	$ 5 71	$ 7 00
Rye, per bbl................	6 72	11 00	— —
Corn meal, per bbl..........	3 58	8 02	6 00
Beef, roast, per lb..........	20	16	12½
Veal, cutlet, per lb	22	17	10
Mutton, leg, per lb..........	16	13	10
Chop, per lb.............	19	14	10
Pork, fresh, per lb..........	18	14	10
Salted, per lb............	22	15	—
Bacon, per lb............	21	20	20
Sausages, per lb........	22	20	12½
Lard, per lb.................	24	20	20
Codfish, dry, per lb.........	9	17	12
Mackerel, pickled, per lb.	14	19	9
Butter, per lb...............	45	47	40
Cheese, per lb..............	21	25	20
Potatoes, per bush..........	66	75	90
Rice, per lb.................	13	12	10
Beans, per lb................	13	08	04
Milk, per qt.................	07	12	10
Eggs, per doz................	33	48	35
Tea, Oolong, per lb.........	1 17	1 04	1 00
Coffee, Rio, green, per lb.	31	24	25
Sugar, good brown, per lb	14	14	13½

GUIDE TO SANTA BARBARA AND VICINITY. 71

	Av'ge price in New England, 1869.	Av'ge price in California, 1869.	Av'ge price in Santa Barbara, 1872.
Sugar, yellow C............	15	16	14
Coffee B...............	17	17	15¼
Molasses, N. O., per gal...	1 03	1 16	75
Syrup,,.....................	1 15	1 25	1 00
Soap, common, per lb.....	12	10	09
Starch, per lb...............	16	22	18
Wood, hard, per cord......	6 96	6 50	6 00
Coal oil, per gal............	48	1 00	75
Shirtings, bleached 4-4, standard quality, per yd	19	20	18
Sheetings, bleached 9-4 standard quality, per yd	43	48	45
Cotton flannel, yer yd....	27	25	25
Tickings, per yd.............	35	33	30
Prints, Merrimac, per yd	15	13	12½
Mousseline de laines, ℔ yd	23	26	25
Satinets, medium, per yd	69	82	...
Boots, men's heavy, ℔ pr	4 66	5 10	5 00

MINERALOGY.

Three miles southeast of Carpenteria the sea shore is covered with a thick deposit of asphaltum, which oozes from the slaty bank in the form of thick tar, covering the beach and concreting the sand and pebbles as hard as rock, running under the sea in places where the surface has become hard and smooth. For many miles along the coast the sea is covered with an iridescent film of oil which finds its way to the surface at numerous points, escaping probably from the out cropping edges of the strata. There are numerous oil springs and petroleum deposits in the county. Sulphur and salt are also found, and some gold and copper in the valley of the Santa Ynez.

Asphaltum is found in several places in the county. At a place six miles west of this town the deposit covers 300 acres from two to three feet thick. Also found at La Purissima and on the Ventura and Santa Clara rivers. Gold is found, of fine quality, at the new mines on Piru Creek, where a number of men are now at work. These mines are, in fact, the oldest in the state, and records are in existence which prove that they were successfully worked so long ago as 1841, seven or eight years prior to the heralded discovery of gold on the coast.

EARTHQUAKES.

The impression is prevalent at the East that life and property are rendered insecure here by reason of frequent earthquakes. Nothing could be further from the truth. The destruction of life in the whole state cannot be compared with that caused by eating hot bread and that American compound called pie. Three times as many persons died of sunstroke in New York city in one day of the present year as have been killed by earthquakes in California since the discovery of gold. No life has been lost, nor any damage done in this county by an earthquake in the last sixty years. The danger is overrated by visitors because definite data have not been published. No records of seismic disturbances previous to 1800 have been discovered, and the archives mention only two years between 1800 and 1850 in which shocks were observed. We give an extract or two from an article on "California Earthquakes" in the *Atlantic Monthly* for March, 1870: "The western slope of the Rocky Mountains, a more important region in point of resources of every description than any other geographical area on the continent, is doubtless to bear within a century a greater population than is now held by the whole area of the United States. Everyone who feels an intelligent interest in the future of our race must be concerned for the prospects of this region. Soil, climate, mineral resources, relation to other great centres of population, alike promise that our children and children's children shall find here all the conditions of prosperity which these features can afford." The writer then proceeds to consider the question of earthquakes as affecting the future resident, giving statistics relative to shocks previous to 1866, from papers by Dr. J. B. Trask, to whom we are indebted for most that is known on this subject. The earthquake of 1812 destroyed the Mission at Santa Ynez, some fifty miles north of Santa Barbara, but the same year brought an even more intense convulsion to the valley of the Mississippi. After that none are recorded until 1850. During the sixteen years from 1850 to 1865, inclusive, fifty shocks were felt at San Francisco, ten at Los Angeles, eight at San Luis Obispo and only six at Santa Barbara. Since 1865 two or three slight shocks have been observed here with the usual result—no damage. The conclusion at which the above writer arrives is that "it cannot legitimately be concluded from the history of that region that the risk is greater than that which is incurred by the inhabitants of the banks of the Mississippi or the shores of Massachusetts Bay."

CALIFORNIA AND PALESTINE.

The similarity of these two countries in very many respects is wonderful. In Deuteronomy viii:8:9 the beautiful land of Judea is described as "a land of wheat and barley and vines and fig trees and pomegranates ; a land of olive oil and honey ; a land wherein thou shall eat bread without scarceness ; thou shalt not lack anything in it; a land whose stones are iron and out of whose hills thou mayest dig brass (copper)." This might have a description of California. In Genesis xxiv:32, Abraham's servant fed his camels "with straw and provender (or barley)." In California the traveler finds no other "feed." Here too as in Palestine are the mulberry and cactus, the wild mustard and the "water-spouts" of David. "The early and latter rain" means little to an Eastern man but a Californian knows the value of spring or autumn rains. When the Jewish prophet promises as a blessing to the favored people, "The treader of grapes shall overtake him that soweth seed" (Amos. ix), and the law says "If ye walk in my statutes the vintage shall reach unto the sowing time" (Lev. xxvi.), and "the plowman shall overtake the reaper," the words describe to the Californian his most fortunate seasons, however unintelligible they may be at the East. "A sweeping rain that leaveth no food" is the too early autumn rain which utterly destroys the pastures; for both in Carmel and California the hills are covered with a kind of "growing hay," a dried grass that is excellent pasture but is rotted by the first rains. "Though the labor of the olive shall fail" (Hab. iii.) is full of force, for no tree requires so little labor. These are but a beginning of the analogies we might draw, did space permit.

The Valley of Santa Barbara.

The following vivid description appeared in the *Overland Monthly*, under the heading "On Foot in Southern California:"

"Above El Rincon the narrow belt behind the strand widens into a fringe of farms, and the mountains become more worthy of the Pacific. There are noble fields, yellow with ripened corn; and brown and russet pastures, running a little way up on the green mountains, as billows run upon the strand. There are long willow hedges; and skeleton pole-fence; red-wood cottages among the fig and mulberries; sweet brooks, let down from the mountain glens by live-oak tethers, across the drought, and creeping weakly through ebony ravines; wide sandy commons of salted grass, close nibbled; white drifted bulwarks, pierced with embrasures, and palisaded atop with reed-grass and enormous rushes; and great brown fields of clotburrs. Elsewhere there are precipitous yellow banks, where the blue ocean heaves its white billows in their ceaseless unrest. On these banks are scattered parks of live-oaks, their trunks salted with vapory whiteness, and stretching their great pallid arms among the green leaves and the pale, pea-green moss, which combs and strokes its long tresses in the beauty of the morning, before the mirror of the sea. What a softness and a mildness these ancient woods put on this Indian summer morning; and the young moss whispers secrets to the gallanting breeze. Beneath this umbrageous canopy I look down between the giant trunks upon the sea, where huge porpoises wallow in the silvery mire of the waters, puffing and bellowing in their lazy tumbles.

"On one side of these ripened farms sleeps the wide Pacific, old Peaceful, purring in his dreams; and on the other, the great green and brown mountains; while over all settles down the tender, white-purple haze of Italy.

"Westward from Santa Barbara the coast belt widens a little more, and becomes a valley. On the outside, along the ocean, there is a graceful ridge, dotted with evergreen verdure of the oak; and through the whole length of the valley, bright groves of the same alternate with the golden and russet ripeness of fields. The very mountains are fruitful with the fatness of the valley; at their summits they display their yellow cores, bursting through rinds of green. All that is celebrated in song or story of Thessalian Tempe, is equaled in this valley of Santa Barbara. Here the hand of winter often forgets through all the months to strew his frost. Here the swelling roots, giving food to man, may be planted and dug in every month of the twelve; and here a fig slip without a root, planted in the ground in spring and watered, has borne and ripened a fig in autumn.

"Just below Santa Barbara the king vine of the cultivated earth has grown and spread itself like a banyan tree, yielding so many thousand bunches at a picking that I dare not mention the number. Here the flocks sometimes forget the times and the seasons; and every month is beautiful with the bleating of lambs. If at times the husbandman could wish the summer sun might touch his fields more lightly, there comes at night a cool, sweet dew from the sea, walking through them like a silent Carthusian, and sowing them with pearly freshness. Here, within sight of these unfading groves, there is perpetual spring. Here is no languishing, no lassitude, no appalling earthquake, and, I had almost written, no death."

For nice Family Groceries, go to C. C. Hunt's.

GO WITH THE CROWD.

C. C. HUNT,
DEALER IN

Fresh Family Groceries

CROCKERY, GLASSWARE, CONFECTIONERY, TOBACCO, CIGARS,

Wood, Willow and Stoneware.

ALSO, A FULL STOCK OF

Standard School Books, Stationery, Notions, Etc.,

STATE STREET.

T. B. CURLEY,

Real Estate Agent

AND

GENERAL AUCTIONEER.

OFFICE: State Street, between Ortega and Cota.

REAL ESTATE BOUGHT AND SOLD AT AUCTION OR PRIVATE SALE.

Fine assortment of Hair Brushes at Apothecaries' Hall.

www.ingramcontent.com/pod-product-compliance
Lightning Source LLC
Chambersburg PA
CBHW031608110426
42742CB00037B/1329